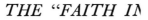

THE "FAITH IN

General Editors: Geoffrey I

GW00854773

DOWN AMONG
THE DEAD MEN

THE STORY OF SALLY TRENCH

Brian Peachment

RMEP

RELIGIOUS AND MORAL EDUCATION PRESS

An Imprint of Arnold-Wheaton

Religious and Moral Education Press
An Imprint of Arnold-Wheaton
Hennock Road, Exeter EX2 8RP

Pergamon Press Ltd
Headington Hill Hall, Oxford OX3 0BW

Pergamon Press Inc.
Maxwell House, Fairview Park, Elmsford, New York 10523

Pergamon Press Canada Ltd
Suite 104, 150 Consumers Road, Willowdale, Ontario M2J 1P9

Pergamon Press (Australia) Pty Ltd
P.O. Box 544, Potts Point, N.S.W. 2011

Pergamon Press GmbH
Hammerweg 6, D-6242 Kronberg, Federal Republic of Germany

First edition 1974
Reprinted 1975, 1978, 1980 (with revisions), 1982, 1984

Printed in Great Britain by A. Wheaton & Co. Ltd, Exeter
ISBN 0 08-017614-3 non net
ISBN 0 08-017615-1 net

DOWN AMONG THE DEAD MEN

The story of Sally Trench

"What's your little game?"
It was 2 o'clock in the morning in the St John's Wood district of London. All was quiet as a lonely policeman walked down the street. Suddenly there was a sound from the darkness above. The sharp beam of the policeman's torch picked out the figure of a young girl, dressed in a sheepskin jacket, wearing rubber boots, and carrying a large haversack, sliding down the drainpipe of one of the houses.

"And what's your little game, Miss?"

"Oh, it's all right, Officer, I live here," said the girl.

"And do you always leave home like that?" The policeman had heard tales like this before. "Let me have a look in that haversack."

The girl opened the bag. Inside he could see packets of cigarettes and a thermos flask.

"I do live here," repeated the girl.

She fumbled inside her bag and brought out a key. "And I can prove it. This is the key to the garage. If you come with me I'll show you my bicycle."

The policeman followed her. She turned the key in the lock, the door swung open and inside was a lady's bicycle.

"Well, why don't you use the front door like everyone

else, instead of climbing down the drainpipe?" The policeman was puzzled.

The girl shrugged her shoulders. "I can't. You see, we have a squeaking stair and my father is a light sleeper. He might hear me."

"I see," said the policeman. "And where are you off to at this time in the morning?"

"To Waterloo Station to look after the down-and-outs," was her strange reply.

The year was 1964. The girl was a brave young woman called Sally Trench.

Despised and rejected

Sally Trench was born in Woking, in 1945. Her father was a rich businessman. At school she behaved so badly that, in the end, the headmistress had to expel her. She started work for the BBC, but her job was not an exciting one; for three months she peeled potatoes and served cups of tea in the staff canteen. Then she followed a six-week course training to be a secretary, and did office work for a while. Later she became a counter assistant in a chemist's shop.

And then something happened which changed her whole way of life.

Walking through Waterloo Station (London) one Sunday night, after a week-end in the country, she bumped into an old woman dressed in rags. Mumbling an apology, Sally walked on. Then she gazed round at 'the dirty drunk old men'—the dossers (tramps), sitting half asleep on the benches. Sally shuddered at the thought of them. She was quite prepared to pass by on the other side and forget all she had seen. And yet, like the dossers, she too had been an outcast. The teachers at school did not like her, and in the same way ordinary people did not like these 'dirty drunken

men'. She suddenly realized how much she had in common with them.

Buying a packet of cigarettes, she picked out two of the scruffiest men she could find and sat down between them. They were both drunk. Too drunk for words. One of them lurched against her. The smell of stale beer was strong on his breath.

"You don't belong here, Missy, not a nice girl like you," said another drunk.

His words gave her the excuse she needed. She stood up, pushed the packet of cigarettes into his hand, and quickly made her way home.

That night, in her bedroom, she made a promise that she would do something to help these people.

Thus began Sally Trench's strange nightly visits. Leaving home at 2 o'clock in the morning, she cycled the six miles to Waterloo Station, carrying food, warm clothing and blankets. She gave them out to the dossers as quickly as possible and returned home at 4 o'clock. Although she was not breaking the law, she dared not hang about too long in case the police noticed her and news of what she was doing reached her father.

"There ain't enough love to go round"

As time passed, she longed to know more about these people, to find out their needs, their hopes and fears. "If only they had a home of their own," she thought, "somewhere where they were free to come and go as they pleased, a place where they would be respected and where they could get back their self-respect." It was then that she heard of The Simon Community Trust.

The Simon Community Trust (named after Simon of Cyrene, who carried the cross for Jesus) was founded in

4

Dossers

1963 by Anton Clifford, who had once been a probation officer. Clifford was concerned with the outcast, the dosser, the junkie and the meths drinker. He believed that the only way to help such people was to find them a home, a place where they could recover a sense of dignity and pride in themselves.

He founded a series of Homes, run by the men themselves. Besides hostels, there was a farm where men who had once been dossers, convicts, and drug addicts worked the land and lived in pleasant surroundings. It was up through these houses, 'the pipeline' as it was called, that the 'outcasts' moved in their struggle back to everyday life. Sally met Clifford and was very impressed. Their ideas were the same. They spoke the same language.

Sally gave up her £18-a-week job to work full-time for the community at Simonlight, one of the houses in a part of London called Stepney. It was here that she came across the meths drinkers, and had what she considered to be her first success. Charlie, as we shall call him, was dying when Sally first discovered him on a bomb-site. The meths had dried out his body like a piece of shrivelled orange-peel.

Each evening she brought him back to Simonlight and nursed him with a mother's care, feeding him on liquids, a teaspoonful at a time. Each evening he made his way back to his bomb-site home, there to undo all the good that Sally had done, with further doses of methylated spirits. His condition became worse and for two days he hovered between life and death. Sally was always by his side, holding his hand, showing him that somebody cared. Just before he died he tried to show his thanks.

"Girl," he said, "yer the first person who's loved me."

To Sally this was reward enough.

For two and a half years she worked at Simonlight, feeding and caring for these unwanted people, until four of the houses had to be closed through lack of money. Sally, worn out from overwork, was bitterly disappointed. Determined not to give up, she decided to carry on the battle on the rat-infested bomb-sites where the meths drinkers live out their last agonizing years.

Rock bottom

Meths drinkers usually begin as alcoholics, that is, heavy drinkers who cannot give up their habit. Out of work and short of money, they buy meths because it is cheaper than ordinary drink.

Sally found that the meths drinkers came from different backgrounds: one had been a doctor, another a priest, many were working-class, and most had once been in the war. Much of their talk was about army life, the last time they had felt like men. It was at this time that many had started drinking heavily because of the tough time they had.

7

Now they were very different: spittle dribbling from the corners of their mouths, their insides burned dry by the meths. Their families no longer wanted them, and they had grown old before their time. They were dirty, unshaven, and had lice on their bodies. A tragic sight for a young girl, like Sally, in love with the joy of living. Death at an early age was their only escape from this living hell. Their homes were the East End bomb-sites where they hung around bonfires drinking themselves into forgetfulness.

Sometimes, because he was drunk, one would roll by accident into the flames, or a spark would set light to a meths-soaked great coat, turning its wearer into a human torch. If he was not burned to death he would be left with terrible marks on his face and body from the burns.

Some lived in the 'derries' (the empty houses waiting to be pulled down), sleeping among the lice and the rats. A fall on one of the rotting staircases could sometimes mean lying for hours in great pain, until help came. Many died of cold, others in drunken fights.

But in spite of bitter hardships, Sally found that the dossers were often kind and warm-hearted, in spite of their occasional outbursts of violence. They knew why people walked by on the other side and they bore no grudge. These were Sally's 'patients'.

On the bomb sites

Each day she 'begged' food and put it in the left-luggage department at Charing Cross Station. Later on in the evening she collected it and made sandwiches in the waiting room. Then she filled her thermos flask with coffee at an all-night refreshment bar on the Embankment, and began her nightly errand of mercy.

9

First she gave the dossers the food, then she cleaned them up, bathed their wounds and drove them to hospital if they needed treatment. She visited those who were in prison.

She ran great risks. Once when she tried to stop a fight the two men turned on her instead and one of them cracked a bottle over her head. Another time she battled her way into a blazing 'derry' to drag a meths drinker to safety.

Before Christmas she worked as a post-office sorter so as to earn enough money to give the dossers a Christmas party. With a borrowed van she toured the 'derries' and bomb-sites collecting down-and-outs and drove them to a central point. There, before a blazing fire, friends handed out sausage rolls and mince pies. Another friend played the trumpet, and hope shone out of sunken faces as they sang carols together. For a brief few hours life seemed worth living again, until the coming of dawn saw them back once more on the bomb-sites.

But Sally did more than just care for their daily needs. She set them a good example. She did not fall into their bad habits. She kept herself clean and tidy. She never smoked, never swore. Each day they knew that she left them to wash and clean up. And gradually there would come a time when, copying her example, some of them too felt the need for a wash.

Long journeys are made up of short steps, and one improvement led to another, until the day when one of them would tell Sally he had decided to 'kick the habit'. He would try to 'dry himself out'. Sally would agree to help him so long as he was sincere. She knew it was no good trying to help those who would not help themselves. But she was prepared to spend endless time and patience on a man who was determined to try. She would sit with him, comforting him, listening to his stories, just being there while he fought off his craving for the bottle. And, if he gave

A night shelter

in, Sally was there to say, "It's all right. When you're ready to have another go, we'll try again." And in two month's time, if he was ready, they would try again, and again, and again, until the battle was won. Sally was there helping men who had been meths drinkers for fifteen years. Sally was always there.

With never a thought for herself

It was while she was recovering from an illness that she first began to think seriously about the effects of the three tough years she had spent on the bomb-sites. "Where am I going?" she asked herself. "How long can I keep up the pace?" She was driving herself to the limit day and night, draining herself of youth and vigour. At this rate, she would end up a burnt-out case, with nothing else to give. The answer, she knew, was another four or five years at the most.

From the beginning she had relied upon her wits, but how long could she hold out? She needed more than just practice in social work in order to succeed. She needed training, too, in order to face the problems that lay ahead.

She began a college course specializing in work with young people. She had spent a great deal of time with young drug addicts and she realized that unless something could be done for them, here were the meths drinkers of the future. Therefore, by understanding the problems facing the teenager in general, and the teenage drug addict in particular, Sally hoped to play her part in helping to stop one of the saddest problems of our time.

Today, Sally is married and has a family of her own. Although much of her time is taken up in being a housewife, she is busy working on a new project—Project Spark. With the help of Leeds Corporation, she has taken over a derelict house (a 'derry'). When repaired it will become a home for young people who, for one reason or another, have no place to go. Six boys at a time—the numbers are kept small so that the boys won't feel uncared for—will spend two years at Project Spark, learning to become adult citizens.

Volunteer cleaning out a 'derry' for use as a community centre

BIOGRAPHICAL NOTES

Sally Trench was born in Woking (Surrey) in 1945, about the end of the last war. After leaving school at 15 she did a variety of jobs. It was in 1962, when she was just 18, that she had her first meeting with the dossers on Waterloo Station. This chance meeting proved to be the start of her nightly visits to help the down-and-outs.

After a year Sally gave up her job to work full-time with the meths drinkers at a Simon Community Home in Stepney, in the East End. The Home had to close because of lack of money. For the next three years she lived on the bomb-sites and in the 'derries', caring for meths drinkers and drug addicts.

Sally began to realize, however, that she could not carry on doing this for the rest of her life—she was rapidly burning herself out. So she left the bomb-sites and wrote the book, *Bury Me in My Boots* (published in 1968) in which she told of her experiences. She then went to college, where she received specialist training in caring for people like dossers, alcoholics and drug addicts.

ACKNOWLEDGEMENTS: The cover photograph is reproduced by courtesy of Sandi Hughes-Jones.
All other photographs are by courtesy of The Cyrenians, Limited.

THINGS TO DO

A Test yourself

Here are some short questions. See if you can remember the
answers from what you have read. Then try to write them down
in a few words.

1 Why was Sally Trench expelled from school?
2 Where did she first meet some of the dossers?
3 After whom was the Simon Community named? Why?
4 How did the Simon Community help dossers?
5 Why were the Community's houses called 'The Pipeline'?
6 Where did Sally first find some meths drinkers?
7 What jobs did some of the dossers once have?
8 Why do meths drinkers sometimes get burned?
9 How did Sally help the dossers on the Embankment?
10 What did Sally do to raise money to continue caring for
these men?

B Think through

These questions need longer answers. Think about them, then
try to write two or three sentences in answer to each one. You
may look up the story again to help you.

1 If you had been Sally's father, what objections might you
have made if you had discovered what she was doing?
2 What made Sally understand a little of how the dossers
felt?
3 Why did Sally finally give up her work with the meths
drinkers?

C To talk about

Here are some questions for you to talk about with each other.
Try to give reasons for what you say or think. Try to find out
all the different opinions which people have about each
question.

1 Why do you think Sally Trench wanted to help these
people?
2 What makes people become alcoholics and meths drinkers?

17

Would it be better for young people not to start drinking at all?

3 What do you think is the best way of helping anyone who has a drink problem?

4 Do you think that people like Sally help others simply because they enjoy it? What keeps them going?

D Find out

Choose one or two of the subjects below and find out all you can about them. Newspapers may be useful, especially local ones, and perhaps you can also look up reference books in your library.

1 *Alcohol* Find out the facts about the drug alcohol. What are its effects? What are the dangers of driving when you have alcohol in your blood? Make a scrap-book of newspaper and magazine cuttings that illustrate these dangers:

Further information is available from some of the addresses below.

2 *Alcoholism* It has been estimated that there are three-quarters of a million alcoholics in Britain today; very few of these become meths drinkers. What is an alcoholic? What problems does he or she have? How does the problem affect the alcoholic's family?

3 *Alcoholics Anonymous* Find out how the AA (Alcoholics Anonymous) began, how it helps its members and which countries it has spread to (the book *AA Comes of Age*, available from the AA, may be useful). Why were the groups Alateen and Al Anon formed? What do they do?

4 *The homeless* For various reasons many alcoholics become homeless and need someone to take care of them. Choose two of the following organisations and find out what sort of help they offer homeless people: Shelter, the Simon Community, the Cyrenians, the Church Army, the Salvation Army.

USEFUL INFORMATION

Addresses

Alcohol Concern
3 Grosvenor Crescent
London SW1X 7EE.

Alcoholics Anonymous
11 Redcliffe Gardens
London SW10 9BG.

British Temperance Society
Stanborough Park
Watford WD2 6JP.

The Health Education Council
78 New Oxford Street
London WC1A 1AN.

Teachers' Advisory Council
on Alcohol and Drug
Education (TACADE)
2 Mount Street
Manchester M2 5NG.

Shelter (National Campaign
for the Homeless)
157 Waterloo Road
London ES1 8UU.

The Simon Community Trust
129 Malden Road
London NW5 4HS.

The Cyrenians
240 Lancaster Road
London W11 4AH.

The Church Army
CSC House
North Circular Road
London NW10 7UG.

The Salvation Army Information
Services
101 Queen Victoria Street
London EC4P 4EP.

N.B. It is best if only one person in each class writes off for information. Remember to enclose a stamped, addressed envelope for the reply. A postal order for at least 50p would also be helpful, if you want plenty of material.

More books to read

Alcohol, by D. Rutherford (TACADE) (P).
Alcohol and Tobacco, by John L. Foster (Edward Arnold, Checkpoint series) (P).
Alcoholism, by Max Glatt (Hodder & Stoughton) (T).
Bury Me in My Boots, by Sally Trench (Hodder & Stoughton) (T).
Caring on Skid Row and *No Fixed Abode*, by Anton Wallach-Clifford (Macmillan), the story of the Simon Community (T).

Finding Out (1) What Happens When I Drink (produced for the Brewers' Society and available from Hobson's Press Ltd, Bateman Street, Cambridge CB2 1LZ) (T).

Shelter, by David Kibble (R.M.E.P., Charities series) (P).

A Short Straight Look at Alcohol, edited by A. Candler (Hope Press Publications, 45 Great Peter Street, London SW1P 3LT) (T).

T = suitable for teachers and olders pupils
P = suitable for younger pupils

Films

Another Little Drink (20 min) and *What's Yours?* (30 min), both colour. Also on video. Suitable for 15-18 years. *The Choice is Yours* (15 min), colour. For 12-14 years. All available from Concord Films Council Ltd, 201 Felixstowe Road, Ipswich, Suffolk IP3 9BJ.

To Your Health and other titles available from The Central Film Library, Chalfont Grove, Gerrards Cross, Bucks SL9 8TN.

Verdict at 1.32 (not suitable for pupils under 14) and other titles available from the British Temperance Society.

Filmstrips

Drinking and Alcoholism (also as slides), from The Slide Centre, 143 Chatham Road, London SW11 6SR.

Drug Abuse (series) – *Alcohol and Health*, available from Fergus Davidson Associates Ltd, 1 Bensham Lane, Croydon, Surrey CR0 2RU.

Video

The Simon Community (30 min), BBC *Open Door* series. Available from the Simon Community Trust. A speaker is also prepared to visit schools, where feasible.

Information packs

Alcohol, from Pictorial Charts Education Trust, 27 Kirchen Road, London W13 0UD.

Free to Choose, from TACADE.